Child-Eyes

Child-Eyes

by

Sarah DeSimone

with illustrations by
Rose Sipperley

The Merry Blacksmith Press
2011

Child-Eyes

© 2011 Sarah DeSimone

Illustrations © 2011 Rose Sipperley

Cover by the PERI Design Team

For information, address:

The Merry Blacksmith Press
70 Lenox Ave.
West Warwick, RI 02893

merryblacksmith.com

Published in the USA by The Merry Blacksmith Press

ISBN—0-61557-035-6
978-0-61557-035-8

To all those who strive to keep learning, searching, and loving with everything they have. May these words bring you understanding, peace, and a flash or two of inspiration.

Table of Contents

Foreword

I FIRST MET SARAH three or four years ago in a coffee shop as part of a developing community group. It is difficult to remember what my initial impressions were at that first meeting, but by the second and third meeting I had become aware that this was a person who, at the tender age of twenty-two, had it surprisingly together. She was deeply involved in her studies, and had a job loaded down with responsibilities. She struck me as being mature and even wise beyond her age, yet at the same time she radiated a child-like joy in life. There was none of that oh-so-hip cynicism that's defined so many of the GenX and beyond generations. There was not that sense of defeat-before-the-race nor unearned entitlement. She knew how to work, and she knew how to have fun.

Her calendar was always full. (Yes, she kept a calendar.)

She mentioned she wrote poetry.

Well, so does the mopey kid down the street. The difference is that the mopey kid will never share his work or seek to develop a voice and a style. He's not interested in maturing or growing as a poet.

Sarah was and is.

I first heard Sarah's poetry for myself a year or two later at a public reading in a different coffee house in a different part of the state. At this point in her life, she had done what I've never seen someone that young do. She had saved her money (I *know*, right?), took the plunge, and quit her job in order to become her own boss. She now works as a freelance editor for several publishers, and writes copy, critiques and abstracts. She's even done some ghost-writing. She's always busy.

But being busy with work didn't mean sacrificing a life. And as a good poet, she's not closeted away from the world, but continues to be a large part of her community, her family, and her friends.

And she is, of course, still writing poetry. Revising. Studying technique. Experimenting. And writing more.

Back when I first heard her read, I was taken by her passion and her use of imagery. I was also amused by her owl fetish. In this book, you will be able to experience that imagery and that passion youself. These are the poems of a young woman embracing life, dealing with it as it comes, the good, the bad, the ugly, and the beautiful. While some poems may strike the reader as very personal, Sarah manages to connect with her reader and forge ties of recognition that span decades and gender—she succeeds at the ultimate mission of every poet—communication.

Furthermore, this is a witnessed journey into adulthood. Through child-eyes. Through carefully wrought poetry.

That is why we're so pleased to be publishing this work.

In addition to Sarah's words, we're very pleased to have this collection include illustrations by the talented Rose Sipperley. Rose is Sarah's long-time partner in crime, and a hugely talented artist. The illustrations you'll see here are only a small part of her skill set. She's also a noted photographer, painter, and sculptor. She's rarely far from her drawing journal which, as anyone who knows her can tell you, is oft-crammed with engaging work. Rose's work in *Child-Eyes* showcases her illustration skills, but that is but one facet. They also work well off the poems. Not an accident.

Sarah and Rose are both people to keep an eye open for.

You heard it here first.

– John Teehan
The MERRY BLACKSMITH PRESS
2011

A Note from the Author

CHILD-EYES IS MY FIRST compilation of poems. Poetry, for me, began as a natural outlet for the frustrations of growing up. Like many young adults, my most profound journeys happened within my own mind. Observing and compiling, deconstructing and experimenting, and trying on this phenomenon everyone called "being an adult". Taking cues from my environment, I found myself dizzy with the expectations and terrified at the thought of failing—or succeeding.

Yet at my unshakable core, I had a firm knowledge of my worth. It rarely reached the surface; but if I dug deep enough, I always found it there. It is my deepest wish that any lost soul who finds this book also finds a little bit of hope between these lines.

It is one of the hardest things in the world to turn inward and understand ourselves. The heart is excellent at protecting us from our fears, our insecurities, and hiding the truth from us. In fact, our friends, our families, and our environment do a great job at "protecting" us from our truth. And we can't blame them. They are only doing what they think is best. They are firm in their belief that the world is a static, unchanging place that will not accept or even allow a difference of opinion. They are stuck in the "that's just the way it is" mentality.

However, there are a few people—and I have been blessed to know more than most—that challenge that way of thinking. They are completely their own person, each value has been carefully cultivated based on what feels right to them, not what friends or family or society gives them. They are strong in their boundaries, comfortable in their skin, and confident in the knowledge that if they continue to help others seek the truth within, we will all be happier and healthier for it.

I don't pretend to have the answers. I'm just learning my own answers—never mind yours! But through my poetry, I hope that you might get a glimpse into my journey and realize we are all going to the same place. We all want the same things: happiness, prosperity, and peace, but the truth of how to get there is wildly different from the person standing next to you—this seems to happen especially when you love the person standing next to you.

Child-Eyes is for all the people that I have met; all the people that I have seen and heard and learned from. You carry with you a small piece of my soul. This is my truth. Please use it to create your own.

Sincerely,

Sarah DeSimone

About the Book

I am finished with lies.
Here, I speak the truth.

I am finished with deceit.
Here, I have no covenants.

I am finished with secrets.
Here are my cards laid down.

I am finished with façades.
This is who I am.

In these pages, you will find pieces of my soul
And here you can learn lessons of my heart.

You will know that you are not alone
And you will know that the world is vast.

And in the end,

We shall be finished with hiding
And finished with fear.

Awakening

The sun rises on a novel day
Something you've never seen before.
You curiously look out the window.
Light becomes tangible
As dreams awaken
And the once impossible
Is not.
Rainbows glitter into existence.
Something you are sure you haven't seen
Since you gave up your child-eyes.
Thumping in your chest
You marvel at your heart.
It lives between abstract and concrete.
Warmer.
As life crashes toward you,
You rush toward it.
One step,
And then another.
The ground is firmer than you remember.
This new day seems no less daunting than yesterday
But you have changed.
Instead of a dodge
You are ready with a strike
Drawing power from conviction
Of a brief moment
Of inspiration.

The Bike Path at Twilight

Warm summer nights
On the roof of your car,
A spunky vehicle, lovingly named,
Vivian: the Volvo of Death.
Hedwig blasting on the side of the road
Proclaiming our twisted view of the world.
Looking out over the water to Providence
Wondering about the lights of the city
And how they held our future.
We'd laugh at the cops as they drove by
Searching for backseat lovers
But we didn't know what love was.
We spoke of life's wonders
Of alcohol and drugs
And girls of course.
We'd giggle ourselves into ecstasy
And spread our joy to the distant reaches of twilight
With the wind in our hair.
We gazed over our kingdom
And saw that it was good.

To See Her for the First Time

We have been friends for a while,
She and I.
We frolicked through snow and ice.
We walked through tall grass.
We fought about peace.
We debated about war.
We explored the crevices of art and science,
Passion and despair.

Then there was the ring.
It appeared one day,
Brilliant as it caught the light
Casting rainbows on the walls
Giving a glimpse into the life I wanted.
The rainbow ring,
It appeared one day
As we sat on a cold gym floor.
She grasped my hands
And confessed to me
My own sins.

Passion Beneath the Surface

A slow burning ember
Buried in the soil.
Smoldering, writhing
Underground
Only to move
An inch of dirt
And the passionate flame
So to leap
And light Creation.

Poseidon's Call

Dare I lay my head upon the sand
That I may dream.
Sweet currents shall wash me
Away.

Dare I see a mermaid
That they may call me crazy
And I, in my naivety,
Believe them.

Dare our worlds collide
And the rumble of the sea
Will either awaken
Or drown us.

On Applying Observations of Nature

An unforgiving soul am I
To steal my courage from the sky.
My speed is from the young roan mare
And strength of ten from the grizzly bear.

My thoughts are from the owl wise.
My stories from the trickster's lies.
With other's voices dare to speak,
The gossip of the bubbling creek.

My patience from the old oak tree,
No one has ever caught on to me!
I snake through life: a slippery eel;
Not one can feel the way I feel.

My shine is from the glistening snow.
My well-made façade is all you may know.
But empty like the grown birds' nest
And dim as the sun sinking into the west.

On Writing Literature

Circumstances dare the hand to write
In ordinary words
No extraordinary order
They can touch our souls
Mere lines on the paper
Feeling so unnatural
Compelled to stop
Desperate for some structure
A clichéd twist at the end
Something for a laugh
Deep and sorrowful humor
Praying for a break in Old English writing
And inverted sentences
Perhaps there is no meaning
Perhaps he wrote it on the toilet
Perhaps he was possessed
Perhaps the word that puzzles the critic
Is one that amused the writer
Perhaps the transition sentence
Hides the heart of prose

The Little Red Flag

The world is a struggle of cause and effect.
Everyone fighting for harmony.
One cause affects another's effect
And the vicious battle is on.

We pull and pull
Like a tug of war
Against everyone who dares pull against us
Trying to reclaim
What we think is rightfully ours.

It is an odd realization
To know this fierce hoarding rages on
And you participate anyway
Because you just can't see another way.

The red flag stays
Always just out of our reach
With the promise of perfection,
Demanding all our strength
And all our lives.

Leaving us to wonder
What would happen if we just let go of the rope?

Thirteen Hundred Miles Away

In the steady wake of time
The waters have torn us apart.
As I'm reaching for you now
I catch my aching heart.

I need to say I love you.
Please, just one more time.
You need to see it written
And listen to the rhyme.

Perhaps it's not so much
Words on acid paper
For they will fade and wither
Dissolving into vapor.

But on a second thought,
This mortal paper speaks
Of a new love's innocent purity
And the wonders that it seeks.

Red ink inscribes our passion.
It may soon turn to grey
But it will match our fading hair
So long after words melt away.

And with it, paper shrinks
Yellow and sepia its tones
But this is the color of memories
And friendship as it grows.

I need you in my arms.
Please, just one more time.
I need to feel you with me
When words are past their prime.

The Question of Certainty:
A Breakdown of Heaven

To question the question of certainty
How is there any certainty at all?
The balance of wisdom and illusion is a pinpoint
There is no way to know which way you have fallen,
Which side you are on.
But hesitancy is the mother of missed opportunity
So shall I miss the opportunity?
Or shall I jump and throw my future at the mercy of the
    Fates?
There is no way to tell if I am right or wrong.
Or if the choice I made followed the morals of this
    universe.
But then again…
There is no morality.
Morality was made my man
And is subject to corruption.
Too easily do we follow illusions,
Too readily do we jump into a stream,
Only to let it carry us softly down the river,
Where the Enemy pools its victims.
But is it the Enemy?
We have the right to choose
Good or evil, light or dark, white or black
Each choice seems more trivial than the last
As the world makes a downward spiral
It is a hall of mirrors, a fun house of illusions.
We think that we feel, but is feeling an illusion?
Of is it thinking that is the illusion?

Are you really thinking what you think you are thinking?
Or is someone or something thinking for you?
These questions receive sneers, rolls of the eyes, and
    outright denial.
A waste of energy to attempt the uncontrollable, yet, what
    is control?
What is the freedom that we so often speak about?
Is there something fundamental to life that we are all
    missing?
And if someone does show up, claiming the secrets of the
    universe,
Will we believe him? Of course not.
There is no direct communication between man and deity.
Everything that cannot be explained is simply labeled
    "mystery."
We rely on man's word to guide us. But where are we
    going?
To the Promised Land?
To a place of no hurt and no sacrifice and no pain?
A land of innocence—
But a land of innocence must be an illusion too.
To keep a man from pain and disappointment and
    suffering
Is to deny him a full life.
Without pain, how shall he understand joy?
But if heaven is a half-life,
There where can we hope to find peace in eternity?

Display

I think it's funny
That you call me vain.
I barely put myself above a pebble some days.
I take the backseat in everything.
You just don't see it that way.

You think this goody-two-shoes thing,
It's the truth, that it's fact.
Shows how much you know
It's all an act; it's really all for you.

Good grades and nice clothes,
Fancy cars and expensive gifts,
I laugh that you don't see
It is all for you.

You are convinced that
The company you keep
Defines who you are.
And because I am closest
I must be the best.

I am not a person to you.
I do not grow in your eyes.
I am a doll
That must keep creating
New and better things everyday.

Heaven forbid
You run out of oil
To preen your feathers with
In front of the other birdies.

Display me,
Stroke me,
Praise me,
And send me to bed.
I will present to you tomorrow
The gold I spun
From the straw in my dreams.

Observations of a Supermarket Cashier

Just use me as a parking meter.
It is rare that people say hi.
Off on their business
With hearts on their sleeves,
They don't realize what they are telling me.

I know that you are unhappy.
I can see you are a binge eater
And your daughter is diabetic.
I know that your son is sneaky
He just stole a candy bar.

I can tell you are in a hurry
And you are going to a birthday party.
You will sign the card in the parking lot
Maybe wrap the present too.
Bows are on aisle twelve.

I know you love Italian food
And your family was from Sicily.
The woman behind you is learning to cook.
She is doing it to please her husband
And to get her kids to eat vegetables.

Oh look, a secret shopper
His kids always look so bored.
They have three other places to go
And his eyes bore into me
As he looks for mistakes.

That woman? She is a closet romantic.
She always looks at those novels
But never buys them.
And he is a vegetarian
But he can't stand tofu or carrot sticks.

Here comes the man who pinches pennies—literally
And this poor woman lives day to day
On three dollars and 15 cents.
She carefully counts her coins
And always gives exact change.

And I can't wait until tomorrow
The coupon lady comes in
She is crazy—but mostly brilliant
Taking fifty dollars off her meals
With her little purple binder.

May I take the next person in line?

That man is a criminal
Security is following him around.
And she is throwing a barbeque.
These people just moved into a new house;
They bought seventeen different spices.

Oy, here comes the grouch
Who will fight me for ten cents.
Next is the sweet old man named Jerry
Who only leaves his house
For chocolate chip ice cream.

Please give me your rewards card, ma'am
You can't get sales without it.
Her confused look tells me
That "no" is a foreign word
And she always gets what she wants.

He is on a diet and she is PMS-ing
And they mix food with sex.
These ladies are from the halfway house.
They are on a strict budget
With exactly thirty dollars each.

I can tell you live in lies
And your kids know it too.
I know he did something wrong;
He picked "I'm sorry" flowers
And those two are celebrating a baby.

You have an oral fixation
And someone just died in his family.
She is afraid of him.
The way her eyes dart back and forth—
And she thinks she can hide behind makeup.

And yet no one notices
If I am there or not.
Go ahead, use me and move on
With barely a goodbye
To your Keeper of Secrets.

Growing Up

Something with chains and flowers
As I walk the line of thorns
And my roots reach deep into the earth
Stealing from your reserves
My green arms stretch wide
And my fibrous belly is full
For I will use you to get ahead
Above the shaded undergrowth
Toward the sun of success
And liberation
With no regard to your hurt
I must press on
Because that is what you did
To your poor predecessor
Because you needed to grow too
Beyond these chains and thorns
To seed yourself with beauty
And kill yourself with heartache

The Mirror
(Self-esteem)

It's in those quick moments
When you are standing in front of the mirror in your red
    underwear and bra,
Chugging a cup of coffee and wishing
That it was 5 a.m.
So maybe you could actually get something productive
    done
Before you enter voluntary slavery
In the service of people who treat you as a piece of
    machinery.
Right there!
After you hiccup from drinking too fast,
You see her in the mirror.
There!

That girl that appears every so often,
That girl you want to be.

She hides in the mirror
Teasing you with possibilities.
She is perfect—
A combination of the sexy tigress
And the playful child.

The light play tricks and your reflection becomes her.
Just a bit more curvaceous, with an even skin tone and
    long, lean muscles.

She is as happy as the last time you saw her (such a long
    time now…)
I've missed you, you say.

She smiles knowingly, with your own smile.
Her white teeth flash and you momentarily forget that
        they are your teeth
As you admire how straight they are.
She twirls in childlike energy and you watch transfixed
As her gorgeous hair bounces to the momentum.
Wide blue eyes sparkle back at you and you feel a flutter
        in your stomach.

There it is; that smile again.

You reach out,
Desperate to merge with her.
Your hand meets the cold metallic surface of the mirror.

No!

You look up and the spell is broken.
You are yourself again.
Sighing, you pull back your frizzy hair into a tight bun
And wish you concealer did a better job of concealing.

Then you realize you're late.

You take one last look in the mirror.
She winks at you before retreating into nothingness.

And you can't help but smile
Because the mirror may play tricks
But it doesn't lie.

Music

Friends torn apart
Hurt and lies
No one would admit
To being my friend
Embarrassed
Because I'm different
I'm quiet
I love openness
And the music that comes with it
While others
Miss the music
Behind black foam
And meaningless gossip
But… maybe
I am meant to be different
Because without the loud hum
Of boys, homework
And things
A piece of the music
Is gone
The buildings fly by
And the bus empties

If Only

I promised myself
One cold morning
That I would never again
Live by if-onlys
And the sun rose
Encouraged by my spirit
So I repeated
I will never again
Live by if-onlys
Light flooded shadows
And truth was revealed
In bright and beautiful colors
Of a new life
And as it moved
Toward the time of no dark
The sun and I danced
Naked and free
Without our if-onlys

The Inspirational Poster

Looking up the mountain
You are sure that you can climb
I mean, the posters say so, don't they?
It sounds right
Working hard
Reach for the moon
Then you fall flat on your face
The world twists in the one way that you didn't anticipate
And you are on the floor
Out for the count
You look up and people look down
You should have known, they say
And you want to kick and scream and punch the wall
But it doesn't do any good
Because you still fell
And how many chances do you really get?
How many times will they tell you to get up
And not to get out?
It's now they start to question your sanity
What made you think you could do this anyway?
A stupid poster?
Crazy girl
And in your sorrow
You are convinced there is a point of light
Something, somewhere
Beyond this
Because reality can't really be like this

Really
Everyone would have killed themselves in despair
There must be another way
So you turn it upside-down
With the hope you'll fall on a star
Or encounter another poster

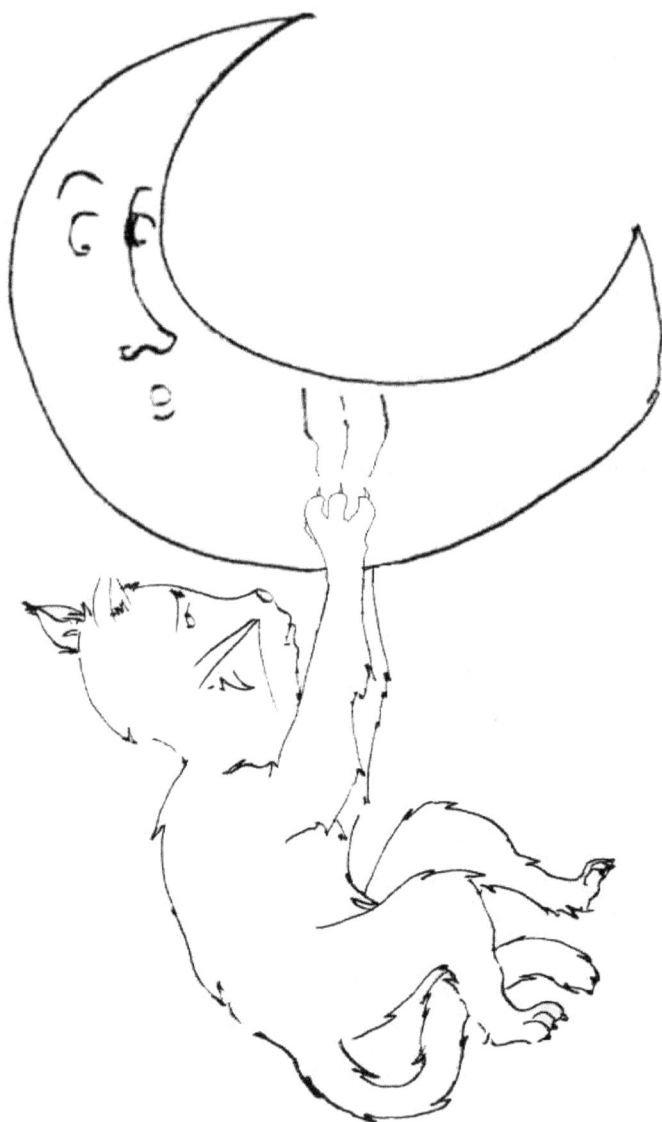

An Imperfect World

I wish I had wings
But perhaps if I did,
I would not appreciate flight.

We call upon the Almighty to solve,
To ease,
But our own temperament suggests
That easy solutions would bore us.

No wonder the Creator
Created an imperfect world,
A giant puzzle for his creation to figure out
To finally seize control.

But what then?
What do you do with a finished puzzle?
You take it apart again
Put it back in the box,
Promising to remember the whole picture.

Perhaps this is why peace lasts so briefly
Peace is a finished puzzle and a finished puzzle is boring.

Complacency in White

I am trapped between my pillow and the clouds
Pressed to suffocation
By soft and fluffy things
Thoughts of the past and childhood dreams
Form droplets of vision
To blur my sight

Drown in feathers
And stale desires
Gasping for some air
And some passion
Feeling like paper, flat and lifeless
With a blank face of no emotion
And this hand squeezing my neck
It seems that it is mine

And in these sheets of days
That surround and coddle me
I find the empty shell of my world
Pale and colorless
My heart tries to escape
Or perhaps, just to beat
As my self-made cocoon of life
Wills me to my death

Of the Same Coin

It is so disconcerting
To find out
That a lie looks exactly like the truth
That right is a twin to wrong.
That the words we used to emphasize truth
Are the same ones we use to emphasize lies.
We would give up our lives for the falsehoods we live
And so we fight to the death
Each convinced of the truths we hold
And the falsehoods too.

Perhaps the Future

I have lived a sheltered life,

Which
Considering

Makes me free

The universe is my playground
So they all told me

I

Am a woman-child
My hips are wide
And my lips are waiting
But my bed is far too small

There is no doubt that I am selfish
I firmly believe that the world is mine
It will conform to me without hesitation
They will all see me coming

There is no doubt that I am vain
I take the compliments I am given
And put them on a pedestal
Look at them! They are mine

I

Am a spectacle
I will dance down the street
I will scream at the top of my lungs
I will not be forgotten

There is no doubt that I am flippant
Duck! My sharp tongue will get you
Do not look at me like that
I have already forgotten what I said

There is no doubt that I am happy
Look at my dazzling smile
Come on let us *enjoy life!*
My goal is to make you happy

I

Am an artist
Tell me your dreams
I will paint you a picture
And create your reality

There is no doubt that I am humble
How dare I speak first?
My talents are far beneath yours
Please do not criticize

There is no doubt that I am generous
You want it? *Take it!*
Take my heart, my coat
Take the other cheek

I

Am a walking contradiction
Do not try to categorize me
Judging yields no results
And labels should be saved for pill bottles

I have lived a privileged life

Which
Considering

Makes me hopeful

The universe is my project
So I came to realize

I

Am here to change the world
And there is no doubt about that

Dark Mirror

In tumult my mind is blank again
Thoughts all scurry to leave
Words through the pen
Are suddenly dead
And what a tangled web we weave

Mere human words don't mean a thing
When dreams have come to call
May the world be kind
If I ever find
The one who never dreams at all

From this midnight window's glow
Peer deadening wide blue eyes
But underneath
The dark is sweet
With ever-twisting lies

Her gaze casts shadows upon the night
Her face as pale as the moon
The flowers wilt
The garden still
With soft approaching doom

How dare you betray the cornerstone!
Says the twinkling star
Fall to the dirt
A frightening hurt
That never leaves a scar

Let's raise our arms together in love
Oh, love, the stuff of heavens be
But if the heavens
Are parts of legends
Where does that leave me?

Monday's Prophecies

I am scared of Sunday night: The beginning of the end.
Because tomorrow I am changed into something I'm not.
The weekend forgets I exist and Monday likes to play
In evil trickster ways, leaving me stranded in the clouds.
Time marches as it tends to do, and the pendulum
      continues to swing
And I am left with the desperate hope that the weekend
      will come again.

Yenta

You should feel…
Equal
No less
Than every second
Of every day
In every moment
And sometimes
Just sometimes…
You should feel superior.

A Prayer in Deafening Silence

In the silence, it is hard not to hear yourself
As a deafening noise that you can't escape from
The funny thing is
You don't really want to
You're fascinated
Scared shitless
And desperately curious
About why this demon torments you

In this silence, you hear the wheels turn in your head
And you know they work—but for your life
You can't find the product of all this turning
You just go round and round in a pitch black room

Then the setting changes and you're up in the clouds
You are bursting with light and you can *feel* love
Burning and bubbling inside you
It makes no sense
Why every moment is a flip of a coin
Heads or tails, light or dark

And you are so sick of trying to find a reason
So frustrated of people demanding a reason
You'd think you would have figured it out
In all of your turning
If there was a reason at all

You think about it day and night
Giving thanks for every happy moment you get
And you focus so hard on being a good person—no,
        a perfect person
So somewhere, some god will look down
And deem you worthy of a life
Without the threat of darkness around every corner

Black Ambrosia

The sun unfurls
Content to rise
After the beep
Warmth descends
And warmth ascends
Saturating my skin
With the aroma of enlightenment
Delicate and harsh
This new day arrives
Sliding down my throat
And soothing my insides
I breathe deeply
And see the possibilities
Lay out before me

Alesa

A smile covers my face
At the mention of your name
And I know everything will be ok.
Suddenly fears are gone
Scattered by your quiet love.

You always have the answer,
My mentor, my friend,
Even if you don't think you do.
And you constantly point the way
To a better future.

You can hear my despair
Before I know I have it.
You catch me before I fall
But you tell me the truth
And you hold up the mirror.

You hear my smiles
From tomorrow's joys
And we laugh to celebrate
This new world that we have founded
With our own hands.

But as much as we have done,
And as much as I will do,
You need to know the truth,
My life would not be as bright
Without you.

Growth of a New Person
(Rosebud)

So slowly
She unfolds
Soft silk
Over sharp spikes
She stretches
From the evil that envelopes her
The sun her guide
Droplets form
On her smooth cheeks
She is free
She is safe
The Ivory Rose
In a field of thorns

The Dance of Pan

Shall we dance?
In a trance?
Afraid of going under…

Shall we flee?
Come with me
Through the trees of wonder…

Shall we play?
Come what may
Imagination asunder…

Let us go!
Who may know?
The path we shall uncover…

Manic State

It swells like a rubber balloon
Makes you float
Without leaving the ground
It is electric and stifling
It is more than one soul can bear
Burst!
Feel it ooze from your insides

They shall flock to you
Moths to the flame
Feeding greedily on your free power
When you are not looking
But you must escape
Run!
Feel the world whipping you into a frenzy

It is exhausting
If you think about it
But why would you?
As the path lays at your feet
Promising the perfect wild ride
Go!
Before the illusion crumbles around you

Pressure
(The Young and Inexperienced)

You think you are more experienced?
I have experienced more
In my short life
Than you have in a lifetime.

The pressure you felt
Is nothing to my load.
This great magnifying glass
Sets my skin aflame.

Talk all you want,
But I could teach you
About living in this world.
This is my world.

I am surrounded
By drugs and drink
By candy colored pills
And fancy smoking plants.

But I am also burdened
By the weight of success
By a letter of acceptance
And a science project.

I must be great, nay, better!
As I am pressed from all sides
And on the top and the bottom
Until I fit in a tiny box.

Is this me? Perhaps for now.
Because it is only here
You allow me to live
Under your precious roof.

But don't be surprised
When I break my bonds
Don't you remember?
You escaped this box too.

To a life where dreams blossomed
And possibilities were many
You ran wild and free
And you tasted happiness.

But darkness grew around you
And now you fear my world.
So you squash my spirit
To protect me from the pressure.

The Confidante

I saw a soul today.
The floodgates opened
And I was found deserving.

Waters rushed around me
As her past was laid before me,
A past that no ear had ever heard before.
I was the first at the gates of enlightenment.

Unhappiness consumes her
And his words bring her down
And in the spark of a smile I can see her.
I can see her.

Fighting desperately against herself
Wishing that her life will change
And she wouldn't have to.

So I tell her the truth—
Not that she hasn't heard it before.
She must be free
And her heart needs to fly again.

It's heavy and it hurts,
This shadow that clouds her soul
And the Gods above pray
That she might finally see the way.

But the sun sets again
On the same old tired world
And she returns to his ego
And his dirty socks.

Freudian Slip

It's funny…
When your mouth starts speaking without your words
And your hands start moving without your actions.
Instinctively this lack of control is disturbing
But, like most things, perhaps we have it backwards.

You see…
We all stand in our own way
It is a baffling fact of life.
We are the best saboteurs of our destiny
And the cleverest storytellers of lies.

Forced Creativity

Forced creativity
Makes awkward and contorted lines
Ugly as can be

So us writer-types
We wait for muses and spirits
To add water to our powder

In silence we despair
Because these ideas squirm within us
And turn stale with time

Edits and cuts make beauty they say
The process never ends on a happy note
Because we drown our darlings

We go to work and drive cars
We pray for any type of sign
To pick up our pens and create a masterpiece

The longer that we wait the staler we become
Brittle and cracked from our parched lips
Digging through to find the spark again

And all our lives are forced creativity
That you can see through broken mirrors
A breathtaking landscape of artistry

Old Soul

I am of an old soul
And an older mind

My memories
Are more archaic than my dreams
My words
Are from ancient echoes

I do not live on the Earth
I am grown from it
Twisting and creeping
Exploring and rising

My feet do not touch the ground
They penetrate it
The fertile soil is my happiness
The barren desert, my wit

I can see the Earth
And her exquisite cycles
Resilient, yet delicate
Hanging on by a thread
And I am saddened

The hawk cries in the distance
My own hoarse cackle
Though my body is young
My heart is the crone

Ancient echoes my guide
Seeing the world through child-eyes

We Are the Lucky Ones

We are the lucky ones
The depressed, the anxious
The OCD, the bipolar
The not-normal

We are the ones lost in our own minds
We are stripped of social constructs
And we are left bare

We are the ones who feel
Deeply, Fully
Untamed and unchecked

We drown in them
And they break open our souls

They twist and turn us
And we tremble under their power

In excruciating misery we carry on
Searching for some peace
Any peace

But we cannot hide from their fury
And they consume us
Affecting everything

We are forced to fight in terror
And we are forced to understand

We are the lucky ones

Boundaries

Guess what.
It's not about you.
You don't have any authority here.
This is my domain.
I make the rules here
And I will do what I like.

Do not misunderstand me.
I love you.
I would lay down my life to save yours.

But right now,
You need to back off.
Because my needs must be met
Especially if they are in conflict with yours.

Guess what.
The world does not revolve around you.
And I shall stand my ground.
This land,
This is my land,
And you have overstepped your bounds.

So step aside
And let me pass
For I am royalty
You taught me that.

The Last Word of Unrequited Love

I loved her, you know.
It was my first love.
It was lustful and quiet;
Passionate and restrained.

Expressed only in a touch,
A hug and the brushing of hands.
Never words
No, the words were too hard
They were too concrete.

If I had said them…well, I did say them.
I tried to say them…
But even if I had said them plainly,
She never would have returned my love.
I didn't deserve her. Not at the time.

Oh, I was jealous of her.
As much as I loved her, I was jealous.
She was everything I wanted to be.
She was so intelligent, so sure.
A quiet gentleness came about her sometimes…
It was when I loved her the most.

But how could she not have known?
It reeked out of me like a foul stench.
I longed to let it out with such force and joy!
But I couldn't.
Instead I pushed it back
So hard I hurt for the years following.
Back into the bottle it came from
Someplace deep in my soul.

"Oh, angst." Spoke the Chosen One

That hurt more than I ever imagined it would.
The Chosen One knew; she was too smart not to notice.
Her flaunted brilliance was something everyone contented
    with.
She was the foil, the opposite of my love.

Not hate, no not hate at all, but apathy.
The Chosen One could not care for my hurt
What looked like a soft fleshy shell
Was really hard leather.
Impenetrable.
So her love was my love's cushion,
And I was not considered.

It is a dull ache, this hurt.
It is with me wherever I go.
It has a sweet sticky taste.
It plays at the back of my tongue.
I use it to take pity on myself.

As I fall into despair,
I throw in a magnifying glass
To blow everything out of proportion.
My imperfections are excuses
A reason for my unrequited love.

"Oh, angst," Spoke the Chosen One.

It seems that if I could only change these surface things,
She would notice me.
Or perhaps, I only want the courage to tell her out loud.

What I am left with
Is a fierce longing for sweet companionship;
Someone that I can be with without fear of anger,
Without fear of rejection.
One who is always ready for a hug, a kiss, a gentle touch
But it seems a hopeless cause.

"Oh, angst." Spoke the Chosen One.

She always seemed to have the last word.

This Grown Up World

I shall never grow up
Because I have seen it
And it is not worthy of me.

In this grown up world,
People do not fly
Their feet are heavy with guilt and shame.

In this grown up world,
The skies are dim
And tears fall in vengeance with the rain.

And why would I join
Such a sad and lonely place
When happiness is my guide?

Poetry

It is not fair
The poetry gets a bad rap
For being simple
Being easier
Novels unroll stories
They make more money
And no one notices
The poem that would change a nation
Is sitting in a trunk somewhere
Bound to acid paper
Fading away
These words must be shared
Your words
My words
Inspiration speaks to the masses
If only we had ears to listen
And tongues to taste the flavor
Of the miracle simile
Of the quiet phrase
And the message of the ages

Perseverance

Absorbed in exhaustion
Weary knowledge ebbs
Back and forth
Half-heartedly grabbing for the smallest tidbit
Iota of fact
Succumbing to the pull of heavy sleep
A long wink
And the whisper of fear to stay awake
The promise of greatness
For one more hour
One more theory
One more sentence as the pencil breaks

The Map

The lines on my hands are deep and bold
There are hundreds, nay, thousands of little paths

Creating landscapes of checkerboards and swirls
Each tiny route tells of a different life

A different choice
Every permutation
And every outcome
Laid out on my wrinkled hands

If only I could read
Such a plainly written map

Lullaby Echoes

Mommy loves you, yes she does…

A sweet echo through the night
As I rock myself to sleep.

Daddy loves you, yes he does…

The chiming of a faint lullaby
As I let go of my waking self.

Auntie loves you, yes she does…

The blankets surround me
In a tight cocoon of affection.

Uncle loves you, yes he does…

It is rare to find a love so consuming
To drown in blissful existence.

Grandma loves you, yes she does…

Guardian angels exist with every step
My shepherds, my relatives, my friends.

Mommy loves you, yes she does…

The Generation Gap

You're screaming in my ear,
But I cannot hear you.
It is not that I am not trying
It just that you are wrong.

My experiences are different than yours
I know you want to protect me.
My experiences are different than yours
Your past cannot define me.

The things that have turned you black
Have given me great light.
Your boundaries, your walls,
They are my pavement
I have much farther to go.

I apologize for leaving you behind,
But I cannot apologize for moving forward.
What you call risk
Is a mere speed bump.
The world is larger than you think.

You say I wear rose-colored glasses.
I say you hide behind stone walls.
You say that safe is better than sorry.
I say safety is relative.

You expect people to hate
So we must treat them accordingly.
I expect people to love
So we must treat them as family.

You know that people do not change.
I know change is all around me.

The chasm between us is vast
And neither is willing to give an inch.

So we exist
In an uneasy peace.
Both of us wishing,
We were on the same side.

Wisdom on a Branch

I was walking in the woods one night
And saw wisdom perched on a branch
In pensive calm we watched each other
Both contemplating our fates
For, you see, I was not supposed to see him
Nor he allow my presence
But there we were, frozen in time
Unable to break the silence
His eyes were bright and wide
And I saw the meaning of life
My fate was decided
All instinct provided
The night I met wisdom on a branch

The Fear of Success

Can I ever escape success?
That horrible creature that follows me everywhere
I fear it
And hide from it
My friends and I delight in outwitting the rascal
But it keeps getting smarter
Discovering my hiding places
I have even pretended to embrace it
Walked with it a while
Only to be a traitor
To sabotage and abandon it
I strive to trick it
To distress it
To force it into giving up
And leaving me alone
But I fear what might happen
If I succeed

The Operation

It's a matter of replacement, he says,
Your brain is worn and bruised.
We must save you with—please,
I know you're confused.

But we must operate now
Or you will die a slow death.
You must consent at once,
Before taking your next breath.

I'm going in, he solemnly says,
To replace those thoughts inside.
I must replace your anger.
I must replace your pride.

An awkward pause, broken by me,
Fine, say I, indignantly.
Onto the bed, I lay down my head.
My brain, it is yours, so shall it be!

He cut off my skull
And he poked at my brain.
Marveling at the sorrows
That he found contained.

He took out the anger.
He took out the pride.
He took out the evils
That I had inside.

And because I had let him,
Trusted him so,
He took everything else,
All that I know.

I felt very dizzy,
Alone, and so scared.
There is no other feeling
That every compared.

He worked on for hours,
Days, weeks, months, and years.
And finally found the end,
The bottom of my fears.

He smiled and said,
That'll do, Little One.
There is nothing more I need,
But I am not quite done.

Then he gave me the birds,
The earth, and the moon.
He gave me the beauty
Of a sunny afternoon.

He sent me the Muses
And music as well.
He gave me true power
And thoughts on which to dwell.

He stuffed them all in
And I thought I would burst.
But he did leave out envy,
Lust, hunger, and thirst.

He gave me the butterflies,
The sun, and the stars.
He gave me the seasons
And he gave me some scars.

He gave me my life,
Renewed and pure again.
He did more than any parent,
Closer than any friend.

And all I had to do,
So simple in retrospect,
Was to surrender my heart,
Mind, soul, and intellect.

Maze of the Owl

Riddle me a tall palm tree
In the middle of a winter storm
And a purple crow on a kitten's toe
That suddenly can't perform

Wings of Angels with Devil horns
And shadows seen in light
Then follow me, the honey bee
To the land of Coke and Sprite

Avoid my eyes, O Brazen One
Or I shall turn you to stone
But never fear, the Gods are here
Before the owl's flown

Intersection

In looking to connect
We travel well-traveled paths
We walk in circles hoping to intersect
Briefly
With someone walking in their circle
Some trample off into the undergrowth
For a bristling change
Uncaring of the poison ivy
Just to brag they have done it

And we miss the trees for the buildings
And we miss enlightenment
Because we are focused on our breath

For a Friend

It's not that I am further along than you
Well, maybe it is
But I know the path that you will take
I walked it too

I don't pretend it will be easy
You will rip yourself apart
Digging and scraping
Fighting to reach the bottom
To find the person that is you

Through layers of things repressed
It's hiding in you somewhere
Impacted and hazy
You need to brave the spiders
And the demons

And at the end of this tunnel
You will see her lying
Shattered and frail
Among the pieces of a broken soul
A living corpse

And she is you
You face each other once again
For so long ago you parted
Left her for the route
Of fewer tears

At this stage one, the chasm is tall
You look up at the light
So far you have to climb
The walls are cold and icy
But you can't be scared to fall

I can't tell you exactly how
It's different for each of us
But I love you
So much
And I just want you to be happy
I know you want that too

But I do know
That one day you will awake
And the sun will shine
And you will not feel
That you are betraying yourself
By greeting the day
With your bright smile

The Call to Light

In the heart of evil, you will find me
Hiding from the light
Wallowing blissfully in my sorrow
Content in endless night
For you see, it is safer here
Why trudge through summer storms
Even if the end is better,
It's not familiar in its forms

    It is true, that good is secondary
    Evil more primary, more pure
    And you cannot buy virtue with a penny
    You need a little bit more
    But these summer storms are passing
    You must come see the light
    The world, your desires, they wait for you
    To leave you endless night

I cannot, will not, emerge
The light is spotted and weak
My dreams sleep peacefully here
And my foolish desires never seek
I shall beat you into a corner
You brash and presumptuous Light!
For I shall win this hour, this day
We shall all embrace the night

I never shall, you know this fact
But neither can you, you see
For you were not made from darkness
And hiding is never the key
Come, I shall cleanse your doubt
And we can weather the storms
After night, the sun shines bright
The Light will leave us warm

Walk Among Hot Coals and Thorns

I am a God
And I am a Devil
I walk where you do not dare

You warn of fire
Unbridled desire
And fix me with your glare

But I am proud
My knowledge enshroud
Joined by a passionate flame

And though you survived
Your existence deprived
By chasing a soul to blame

So do not say
Your way is the way
Or that I should heed your cries

Because I am a God
And I am a Devil
And all Creation has made me wise

The Universe Encompassed

In the beginning there was the Word
And the Word was God and within God
And she proclaimed from the throne
That order comes from chaos
And future from the past
So to create an Earth of color and variety
In which silly creatures walk
Contemplating their purpose
Creating chaos
So to create the Word
That has existed from the beginning

Fresh Breath

There is dirt under my fingernails
I begin to wonder what beauty was
And can we fall in love with chaos?

I rejoice in the order that chaos brings
Bathing in the sunlight of stardust
And dust bunnies

I gnaw slowly on a mint leaf
Plucked with my stained fingertips
It tingles my tongue

I fear for the future
As much as anyone

Sticking my nose into a hibiscus
I cross my eyes to see pollen
And wonder about microcosms

But the petals are satin on my cheeks
And I must be content

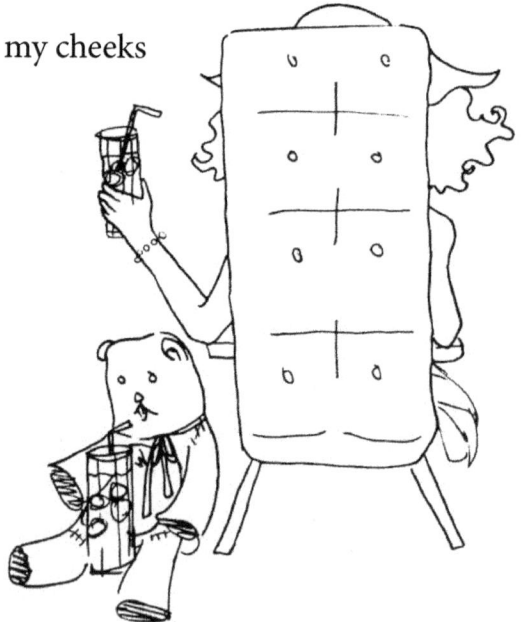

What You Gave to Me

You spent so long telling me to be smart,
To be independent,
To go off and make something of myself.
Well, I am.

You spent hours upon hours trying to toughen me up,
To make me invincible,
To make me better than any enemy I find,
Well, I am.

You spent years teaching me to be wise,
To get me through the fire,
To propel me past all obstacles.
Well, I am.

The world that you wanted for me does not exist,
But you taught me strength.
You gave me wisdom and knowledge
So I will have to build the world again.

Exploring the Structure of the World

Looking up,
Looking down,
Looking around at life spread before me.

Glory lost,
Glory gained,
Glory in the enemy and the secret friend.

Cold as fire,
Cold as ice,
Cold eyes cast judgment upon the unknowing.

Justice given,
Justice taken,
Justice forcing the hands of good and evil.

Strength of mind,
Strength of spirit,
Strength in the hearts of the downtrodden.

Tasting sweet,
Tasting bitter,
Tasting the palate of darkened old wounds.

Warmth of love,
Warmth of hate,
Warmth of a body lying next to me.

Faithful words,
Faithful acts,
Faithful wants in the souls of non-believers.

Searching high,
Searching low,
Searching for something right under my nose.

Child-Eyes

As I look through my child-eyes
I see what you have forgotten
I feel what you dulled senses cannot
And I grow further than you ever could
My innocence unbroken
And I feel deeper than you ever though possible
But you are not interested in the depths
You have wants that have festered into needs
But I have not forgotten
Come to me
Oh, grown up ones
For you do not hold the key to happiness
Here is your ice cream
Here is your teddy bear
Follow me to eternal life

About the Author

Sarah Fawn DeSimone is an editor, author, artist, philosopher, and perpetual student of human nature. She is a proud Rhode Islander and is slightly obsessed with owls.

photo by Rose Sipperley

About the Artist

Rose Sipperley is a painter, sculptor, and all-around artist who can create vivid and powerful artwork with whatever she happens to have handy. She is an Art History snob and a proud Rhode Island transplant.

photo by Rose Sipperley

More Fine Poetry
from
The Merry Blacksmith Press

Albany: an Autobio in Poemtry
by Ben Ohmart

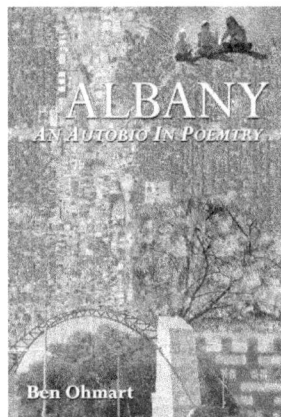

where I'm coming from
by Jay Walker

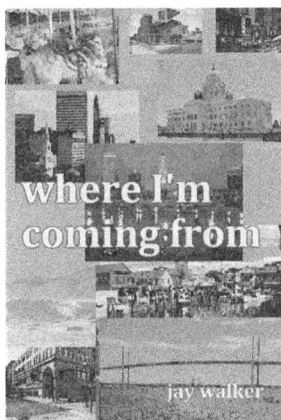

flower
by Jay Walker

Dear Night
by Christopher Calvert
(coming in 2012)

www.merryblacksmith.com

www.ingramcontent.com/pod-product-compliance
Lightning Source LLC
Chambersburg PA
CBHW062017040426

42447CB00010B/2032